5S

FOUNDATION FOR PERSONAL AND BUSINESS EXCELLENCE

A WISDOM VILLAGE PRESENTATION

Books from Wisdom Village Publications envision to enhance and enrich their readers with life changing experiences from the business, mind, body and soul genres. They strive towards holistic development.

Editorial Coordinator Anu Anand

ISBN 978 93 80710 235

Published in 2012 by:

Wisdom Village Publications Pvt Ltd
Knowledge is information. Wisdom is transformation.

649, O4U, Udyog Vihar, Phase V, Gurgaon, Haryana-122001
www.wvpd.in

To Book Your Orders:
Email: wvpdindia@gmail.com
Or Call: +91 9810800469

Published by Anu Anand;
Cover Design and Page Setting by Sunil Mathur;
Printed by JK Offset Graphics (P) Ltd, B-278, O.I.A, Phase-1, New Delhi-20.

5S FOUNDATION FOR PERSONAL AND BUSINESS EXCELLENCE

Kailash N. Anand
Rai Chowdhary

Wisdom Village Publications Pvt Ltd

W V P D Knowledge is information. Wisdom is transformation.

Foreword

The concept of 5-S has been developed by the Japanese, based essentially on the housekeeping system. It contains five words, all of which begin with the letter "S". Basically 5-S revolves around maintaining orderliness and cleanliness in workplace. Cleanliness leads to a safe and pleasant workplace. Orderliness results in better utilization of workspace, and reduces waste at the same time.

5-S is recognized as the first step in implementation of Lean and TQM tools in any organization. The application of 5-S is known to have dramatic results in improving quality and productivity. Because it is simple to use and apply, quite often managements tend to ignore it. There is a tendency to focus on more elaborate programs like Six Sigma, Balanced Scorecard etc. in expectation of better results. However, the reality is that 5-S is one of the foundation stones of successful organizations and contributes significantly to its improvements at all levels. In manufacturing plants, offices, and service organizations, so much time is wasted in searching for things such as tools, forms, documents, gloves, wiping cloths, gauges, fixtures, etc. Implementing 5-S delivers immediate results by eliminating such waste, reducing defects, delays, breakdowns, and improving safety, all translating to lower costs.

This book by Kailash N. Anand and Rai Chowdhary has brought out these concepts in a very lucid manner with pictures and number of examples from different areas. A step-by-step approach with a proper roadmap makes the concepts easier to understand and implement. It is a simple and effective book for helping everyone who wish to work efficiently by adopting 5-S.

Dr. Giridhar Gyani
Secretary General,
Quality Council of India

About the book

This book is written to introduce you to 5-S – foundation for personal and business excellence. The term **5-S** comes from five Japanese words associated with the methodology of organizing and managing a work place to produce better results faster.

The word 'Excellence' is synonymous with 'Working Smarter' and it is important everywhere, whether it is a shop, an office, a factory or at home and to everyone. Excellence in processes automatically results in production of quality goods and services with minimum effort and on time.

It is applicable to various sectors such as manufacturing, information technology, product design, health care, services in both government and private sectors. It is found that real value added work is a tiny fraction of the total time taken to complete a given task (often under 10%). This means there is a huge opportunity to improve. A simple and effective way to get started is by adopting 5-S discipline in day to day work. It does not require complex analysis, and can be practiced by everyone regardless of occupation and position. 5-S addresses the basic issues that otherwise could hinder working smartly. In brief, it is the foundation on which Personal and Business Excellence is built.

We trust you will find it practical and easy to understand. In the spirit of continuous improvement, we invite you to share your ideas for future editions. We shall acknowledge the same.

Thanks!

Kailash N.Anand
knaisi@hotmail.com

Rai Chowdhary
rai_chowdhary@yahoo.com

Acknowledgments

The authors would like to thank the American Society for Quality (ASQ), USA for permission to reproduce an article by Mrs. Davorka Filipusic on "5-S for Families" published in the May 2007 issue of Quality Progress. The authors are also grateful to Dr. Giridhar Gyani - Secretary General, Quality Council of India for writing the Foreword and to Mr. Avik Mitra, Advisor, Quality Council of India, for his valuable suggestions. Thanks are also due to Mrs. Shobha Ahuja, Mrs. Sucharita Anand and Ms. Vanaja Ratnam for providing editorial assistance.

Contents

Chapter 1

What is 5-S

The term 5-S represents five Japanese words.
These are:
Seiri
Seiton
Seiso
Seiketsu
Shitsuke

Let us look at each "S" and understand what it means.

Seiri – Sort or Segregation

This implies removal of unnecessary items from the
workplace and retaining only what is needed.

Removal of unwanted
items/documents

Removal of unwanted items/documents

Seiton – Store / Systematic Arrangement

Arranging the required items in an orderly manner so that they are found quickly.

Orderly arrangement of tools   *Orderly arrangement of books and files*

Seiso – Shine or Clean

Systematic cleaning of the work area so it is easy to see what goes where, and the area is neat and tidy.

Cleaning operation in an office

Sieketsu – Standardize the first three S's

Ensure that everyone does the first three S's using a Standard approach.

	Standard defines the following					
	How frequently	How to	Who	What areas	Where	How much
Sort						
Store						
Shine						

Shitsuke – Sustain/Discipline

Keep up the effort and do 5-S regularly.

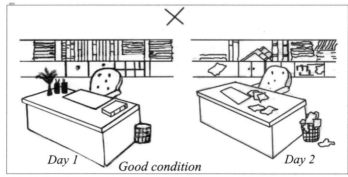

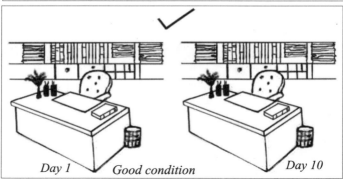

If you notice carefully – each S builds on the other; as such you can think of these as phases. For example, it would not make sense to start the second S i.e. Store unless you have done Sort. There is no point storing things that are not needed. Further, if you don't do the third S i.e. Clean, you may have trouble finding things at a later date.

Chapter 2

Why 5-S

Business today is becoming increasingly challenging, and every organization will have to learn how to be lean and deliver quality, especially so at this point of time, when survival of many industries is at risk. In this process, 5-S can help considerably by improving efficiency and quality.

Taken to a deeper level, if 5-S can become a way of life it can transform organizations.

Time spent in looking for an item, or a piece of information is non-value added. It drains you and your company. The implementation of 5-S addresses this issue directly, and allows employees at all levels to take ownership and action. Along with the implementation comes better utilization of space. This directly contributes to the financial health of the organization.

5-S is actually a natural process — you can see it occurring in nature effortlessly. We also practice 5-S in our daily routines — bathing, dental care, etc. are all part of 5-S at the personal level. We need to extend this to work, and make it a part of the way work gets done.

When employees and customers at several companies were asked what they want to see in an ideal workplace – here is what they said:

- Clean, safe, conducive and pleasant work environment
- Tidy with efficient use of space and other assets
- Easy to find materials, tools, equipment, documents
- Enable easy and timely identification and correction of errors
- Easy communication with visual displays and aids
- Deliver good quality services and products
- Positive changes in attitudes
- Improved time management and efficiency in service delivery
- Vibrant team spirit

5-S plays a significant role in each of the above, thus improving organizational and individual performance at many levels, and in many ways.

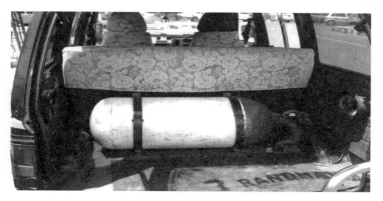

Unsafe condition – Improper storage of gas tank
Violation of 2nd S

Chapter 3

Where do you Stand in 5-S

Using a simple three point scale you can get an estimate of where you stand in 5-S. One might ask why should I measure – the reason you would want to measure is so that you can make improvements and track your progress.

Consider these three scenarios at a workplace:

Scenario – 1

All items are arranged in proper order with labels and there are no unwanted items around. Once an item is taken by an employee, he takes the responsibility to

Excellent Workplace

9

bring it back to the right place and hence no time is wasted in searching. There is no contamination / dirt affecting the work area adversely and there is no littering of trash. Everyone does their part in keeping the work area clean and tidy.

Scenario – 2

People litter the work place. Some things are not in their designated places.

Good Workplace

Scenario – 3

Everyone acts irresponsibly and throws things around.
There is practically no housekeeping. Much time is lost
in searching for things. Workplace is untidy with dust,
dirt, grime and trash piling up.

Bad Workplace

Ask yourself – which scenario does your workplace resemble the most?

If you do this for each of the work areas (or
departments) in your organization or company and

calculate the average score – you will know where you stand. Moreover, if this metric is displayed on a board for everyone to see, together with pictures of work areas – and their scores – it can act as a powerful catalyst for change. Including a benchmark helps by illustrating what other leading organizations have achieved.

Benchmark Average = 4.3	5-S Score Tracking (as of 4/5/06): goal>=3.0					
	Dept 112	Dept 113	Dept 114	Dept 115	Dept 116	Plant Avg
Sort	3.6	2.7	4.2	3.4	4.1	3.6
Store	3.2	3.1	4.4	3.9	4.4	3.8
Shine	3.8	3.3	4.3	2.8	3.1	3.5
Standardize	2.1	3.7	4.0	4.6	2.3	3.3
Sustain	1.0	2.8	2.8	2.6	2.8	2.4
Avg by Dept:	2.7	3.1	3.9	3.5	3.3	3.3

Interpretation of the metrics:
- All departments are lagging the benchmark
- All departments are weak on Sustain; below goal
- Dept 112 average is below Goal; others are achieving minimum goal required
- Dept 113 has 3.7 in Standardize and is below goal of 2.7 for Sort; need to take a deeper look at what is being standardized

Let us now focus on each S in some depth.

Chapter 4

First S – Seiri or Sort

Remove unnecessary items; keep what is needed, and in quantities for immediate use only.

Over a period of time you will find things tend to accumulate in your work area creating a clutter, and most of them are seldom used. They lie around taking up space, making it hard to find the ones you really need and often cause safety hazards. Sorting them out into what is needed and what is not – is therefore a good starting point.

Here are the steps to follow:

1. **Identify the things that are no longer useful and remove them from the work area**

   Examples: Outdated diaries, files, pens without ink, broken chairs, empty fuel cans, worn out or damaged tools, scrap, obsolete computers, expired medicines, etc. These are things that are not useful to you and cannot be used by others either. These need to be removed and sent for recycling or discarded as trash.

2. Red Tagging

Classify the remaining material into three categories:

    A. Useful and necessary for immediate use

    B. Useful but needed for future use

    C. Usable but not in this work area

Keep the items in A at the work place. Put Red Tags (see graphic for example of a Red Tag) on items in B and C categories.

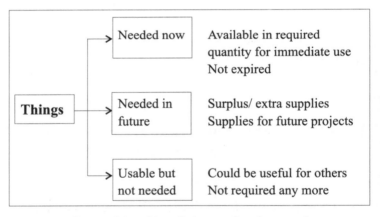

Categorizing things being used and not used

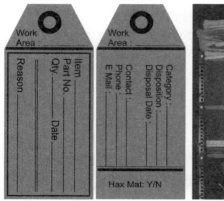

Red Tag

Red Tagged items in a cupboard

3. Evaluate Red Tagged Items

Once the items are red tagged they are evaluated for appropriate action such as:

- ▸ Moving to another location in the work area

- ▸ Storing items away from the work area

- ▸ Transferring to a central Red Tag Holding Area

- ▸ Disposing off

4. Disposal

At this point one would be left with items that are useful but not for this work area, and possibly not for the organization either. Examples might be obsolete computers, printers, equipment, surplus office equipment, tools etc. These items can be:

► Scrapped

► Recycled

► Sold / auctioned

► Made available to others who may want it

► Gifted to a school, college, or other institution

Red Tag Holding Area

Create a specific area for holding Red Tagged items. It should be a place where other people can come and see what is available for disposal. Make sure the Red Tags have a final date of disposition on them otherwise this area will become a long term dumping yard consuming precious space and resources. Many companies are also creating an electronic Red Tag Holding Area so the items available for disposal can be easily seen by anyone across the company.

This leaves us with items that we need to do something with; so we will move to the next phase which is the second S.

Chapter 5

Second S – Seiton or Store

A place for everything and everything in its place.

Having a proper place for everything eliminates clutter and makes it easier to find items when they are needed. This also prevents re-ordering of things just because you could not find the one you were looking for.

Here are the steps to follow:

1. Location

Identify the location for the items you will need at your workplace. In this step you are not doing a detailed layout, but a general map of what goes where – for example, you may want all your cutting tools in the front, operating manuals on a shelf to your left, test guages on a bench behind the work area etc.

2. Best Location

Use the 80/20 rule as a guide based on consumption to decide the proximity for each location; you will find that only some items (about

20%) are used most often (about 80% of the time). These should be closest to the point of use. Here are some more points to consider:

- ► Items not needed frequently can be stored at a short distance but should be accessible quickly
- ► Items used together should be grouped and stored close to each other
- ► Process of picking and returning to its original place should be mistake proof. Use automation if possible, for example – hanging tools on a self-winding chord
- ► Access space to pick up items and return should be adequate to prevent accidents and injuries
- ► Think of the function and sequence in which items might be needed; use that as a guide in space layout

Category	Target	Suggested Method
Spaces	floors, walkways, work areas, walls, shelves, warehouses	Demarcate space
Products	raw materials, finished and semi-finished parts and products	Storage bins, racks etc.
Equipment	machines, equipment, jigs, tools, instruments, gauges, dies	Installation places marked, storage area/ equipment decided
Furniture	work tables, chairs, cabinets, racks	Demarcate the place of use
Transportation tools / spares	carts, pallets, conveyer	Create and identify location for storage

Orderliness targets

3. Labeling

Identify the locations using good visuals so they are easy to find. Create standardized labels and signboards to identify what items go where both for the user and also for those who will re-stock the supplies. Make it easy to see how much material is there and when it is time to replenish. Given below is a sample titling for materials and their location.

Things / Items	Location
Fevicol, stapler and clips	Drawer 1
Paper, files and folders	Drawer 2
Blueprint / drawings	Cupboard 1
Personal files	Cupboard 2

Item and location label

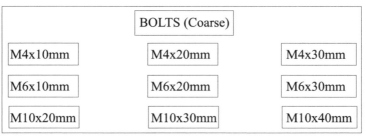

Item, size and location label

Disorderly arrangement

Orderly arrangement as per shapes of the items

Chapter 6

Third S – Seiso or Shine

Clean the workplace and the materials thoroughly so there is no dust, dirt or grime anywhere. Make cleaning a routine part of work and ensure it is done regularly.

It is important that every employee develops a sense of pride in his workplace for its cleanliness. Initially it might take some effort. However, over a period of time, it will spread across the organization and become part of its work environment and culture.

Here are a few steps that could help in achieving this:

1. Determine Shine Targets

Identify what items and areas will need attention – warehouse items, equipment and furniture, floor, windows, walls, cupboards, drawers, curtains, office areas, etc.

2. Assign Responsibilities

Divide the areas and items into manageable chunks and assign to individuals. If your organization is mature enough, let people volunteer themselves and take ownership. In some cases you may need extra manpower to accomplish this the first time; However, subsequently this need would be minimal.

3. Shine Method

Make sure there is a consistent method, right tools, and right supplies are used for cleaning purposes. Here are some points to keep in mind:

- ▶ Define the cleaning process for each item and area that needs cleaning, train people in the use of right tools and supplies ensuring that all functions are maintained post cleaning
- ▶ Establish a regular schedule and entrust a responsible person with the same
- ▶ Make it a part of their job requirements and set up a tracking system using a visual chart showing what item and area was cleaned and when. Provide space for date, and initials of the person responsible for the area

Sample Shine Targets and Areas

Targets and Areas	Check off		Comments
	Yes	No	
I-Inventory Items			
Have you removed all dirt and dust from products, parts and/or materials, storage shelves and pallets?			
II-Equipment			
Have you removed dust, dirt, oil stains & finger smudges from:			
1. Vicinity of the equipment, underneath the equipment, top of the equipment, inside the equipment cover?			
2. Pneumatic pipes and electrical cables?			
III-Spaces			
Have you removed sand, dirt, dust, trash, water and oil puddles from floor spaces and walkways, ceilings and beams, light tubes and bulbs?			
IV-Office			
Have you removed dust, dirt etc. from:			
1. Leg of the chair, underneath of the table			
2. Top and inside of the shelves/ cabinet, curtains, carpets			
3. Computer, printer, keyboard, CPU and other accessories			

4. Tools for Shine

Use the right tools and materials for cleaning. They can help get the job done quickly and efficiently – however, be careful – they can also result in serious problems.

In one case a paint manufacturer had to scrap lakhs of litres of yellow paint due to contamination coming from the equipment used for cleaning their tanks.

The principles of 5-S can be applied to the tools and equipment for cleaning. Store them in such a way that they are easy to find, use and return.

5. Shine

The actual act of cleaning is where it all comes together. People responsible for doing this need to be considered just as valuable as others who are building products or providing services. There is more that happens as cleaning work begins – consider the following:

▸ Ensure that a standard or benchmark is available so it is clear what level of cleaning is acceptable

- Make sure that a schedule has been set and is adhered to
- Be observant of leaks, missing parts, equipment, things out of place, color changes, odors, sounds etc. because these might be indicators of other serious conditions that might need attention
- Use touch (where safe) to detect unusual conditions

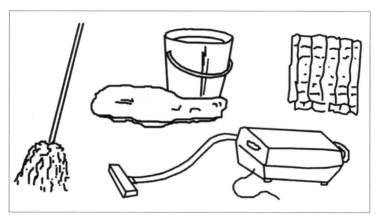

Cleaning tools

25

Chapter 7

Fourth S – Seiketsu or Standardize

Ensure that the first 3 S's are conducted in a standard manner.

Having done the first 3 S's, by now your workplace should be looking very clean, tidy, and presentable. However, these gains can be lost because conditions tend to degenerate over time. To prevent this from happening, we practice the Fourth S, so that the first three become part of our routine and habit.

A simple system is required to make this happen – one that will identify who does what, and when. Some means to motivate people might help too – interdepartmental competitions, or bench marking visits can be conducted as well.

Here are a few steps that will help in standardizing the processes:

1. Assign Responsibilities

Everyone needs to have a role and know what it is. They also should be clear on when and where to do the first three S's, and, have the appropriate training and tools for the same.

2. Integrate the first 3 S's

Make them a part of the expected or standard work for all employees and hold them accountable for getting these done.

3. Monitor Regularly

Conduct audits to assess compliance with standard work. Use a 5-point scale (for each of the 3 S's) as shown below to evaluate performance. Make it known that this measurement is being used, and, if possible, display their performance on a visual board for every one to see.

Five Point Scale for Sort

No.	Description	Level	Score
1	Needed and un-needed items are mixed up at the work place	Worst	1
2	It is difficult to distinguish between what is needed, and what is not	Bad	2
3	Anyone can easily distinguish the needed from the un-needed items	Average	3
4	All un-needed items are stored away from the workplace	Good	4
5	Un-needed item have been disposed off, and only needed items are at the work area	Best	5

Five Point Scale for Store

No.	Description	Level	Score
1	It is impossible to know which item is kept where and in what quantity	Worst	1
2	It is possible to locate items after searching for a long time	Bad	2
3	It is possible to locate items fairly quickly	Average	3
4	Most items and their locations are identified by labels and can be retrieved without any delays	Good	4
5	All items are always available at identified locations, proper labels are present	Best	5

Five Point Scale for Shine

No.	Description	Level	Score
1	The work place is filthy and has not been cleaned in ages	Worst	1
2	The work place is cleaned once in a while, and is very dirty	Bad	2
3	Work place is cleaned periodically, but there is still evidence of dirt and grime	Average	3
4	Work place is cleaned periodically, there is no evidence of dirt, dust, or grime	Good	4
5	Cleanliness is part of standard work, it is audited regularly, and preventive measures are in place	Best	5

NOTES:

1. Each of the above scales need to be used progressively. Thus, if criteria for a previous rating are not met, the next level rating cannot be assigned. For example – cleanliness may be a part of standard work and audited, however the work place is only cleaned once in a while and is very dirty. Therefore, the assigned score would be 2 instead of 5.

2. You will find the terms used for the criteria in the scales above are somewhat subjective (very dirty vs. evidence of dirt, etc.). This is unavoidable because we cannot set universal standards that will fit every industry and every business. What is very clean for a brick manufacturing plant would be considered very unclean for a milk processing plant.

3. You will need to adapt the tables to fit your requirements. Therefore, please add specific measures and descriptors that will work for you. For example, in very high precision components and semi conductors processing, contaminant level standards are very stringent (<3600 particles of >=0.5 microns per cubic meter) and defined by class levels. If such standards are available for your industry, they must be

integrated with the scales provided.

In addition to the above-mentioned scales, you will also benefit from using a schedule to monitor/audit. An example of such a Monitoring Checklist is provided below for your use. Again, you might consider adapting it to fit your exact needs.

Monitoring Checklist   Auditor:_____Date_____

5-S Phase	Check Point	Rank (1=Worst 5=Best)	Initials of Auditors	Comments
Remove un-necessary items				
Sort	Have all un-needed items been removed?			
	Are passage ways and work areas clearly outlined?			
	Do un-needed items have Red Tags, and are they filled out?			
A place for everything and everything in its place				
Store	Is everything at its assigned place?			
	Are shelves, tables, cleaning tools placed in orderly manner?			
	Are hoses, cords, cables, O Rings, and tools properly arranged?			

	Keep everything and every place shining			
Shine	Are exhausts, filters, and ventilations in good working condition?			
	Are all work areas clean/shiny?			
	Are the machines, equipment, and work areas clean/shiny?			
	Ensure the first 3 S's are conducted in a Standard manner			
Standard-ize	Does everyone know his or her role and responsibility?			
	Are the processes, tools, and equipment for Sorting, Storing and Shining standardized?			
	Is a standard evaluation scale in use?			
	Integrate these practices as a regular part of work			
Sust-ain	Is 5-S periodically discussed at department meetings across levels?			
	Is 5-S a part of job description for all?			

4. Prevent Root Causes

While doing the first 3 S's is a good idea, we must understand that it is corrective in nature. To make significant progress, one must think in terms of prevention. To that end, here are some questions that can help us shift from a corrective to preventive mindset:

- ▸ Corrective: Sort out the mixed items
  Preventive: Do not let items get mixed up

- ▸ Corrective: Arrange disorderly things properly
  Preventive: Put things in the right place to begin with

- ▸ Corrective: Clean floors every day
  Preventive: Prevent floors from getting dirty

NOTE: It must be understood that Corrective Actions often are within the span of control of local employees and supervisors in the workplace. Preventive measures may require working on the system, therefore senior management will need to be engaged and committed.

Chapter 8

Fifth S – Shitsuke
or Sustain

Integrate the mentioned practices in previous chapters as regular part of work at all levels.

Of all the S's this one is by far the most difficult. Creating a systemic change is hard to do without demonstrated commitment from the organization's managers and leaders. It is therefore important that all ranks of management and leadership get involved and lead by example. Then 5-S can become part of everyone's job, and a sustainable shift to internalizing 5-S will begin.

Sustaining the gains becomes easy if everyone realizes their importance and feels the need. We keep our homes organized and clean, why can't we keep the workplace organized and clean? A change in mindset and habit is needed. A beautiful, organized and clean workplace can make it more pleasant to work.

The steps to Sustain can be summarized as follows:

1. Awareness

Everyone should be aware of the importance and

benefits of 5-S. Management and leadership should demonstrate support via words and actions.

2.   Time

Adequate time should be allotted in the work schedule to perform 5-S.

3.   Structure

A structure in the organization helps ensure how and when 5-S activities will be phased into different areas, and implemented across the organization. As such a Steering Committee, and few 5-S Teams in the beginning can be helpful in this regard.

4.   Support and Commitment

Leadership and Management support is crucial to get the effort started and will play a vital role in sustaining the same. They will need to lead by example; once their direct reports are convinced that the support is there, it is easier for that support to flow down further into the organization.

5. Reward and Recognition

Adequate rewards and recognitions should be in place for starting the 5-S effort, and also for sustaining it on a regular basis. Together these go a long way in driving the right behaviors and preventing slipping back to old habits.

6. Satisfaction and Excitement

Make the implementation and conduct of 5-S enjoyable this will generate positive mindsets, which can spread and build more involvement. An annual or bi-annual event where people present their benefits and also discuss challenges faced in this journey will help groups learn from one another and create their own support networks.

Chapter 9

Road Map for Implementation

We discussed earlier that implementation of 5-S can be thought in terms of phases. Here we discuss in detail about the types of actions needed in each phase. The steps shown below are typical and you might need to adapt them for your organization. Ahead of the start of the 5-S implementation, there is a planning phase, and that is discussed first.

Planning Steps:

1. Briefing senior management on 5-S, and its value to the organization

2. Setting up a team for 5-S implementation; this may comprise of Steering Committee, Conveners, Promotion Council, Audit Team, and others as necessary

3. Divide the total (inside and outside) area into zones. Decide the priority zone and groups that will be involved in 5-S implementation of that zone, together with leaders and members

4. Announce the start of the 5-S journey for the organization this needs to come from the head of the organization (President or CEO) to all employees of the company

5. Prepare a 5-S policy statement

6. Prepare a deployment plan for selected areas together with roles, responsibilities, and deadlines for phase completion

7. Design and print Red Tags, distribute to respective area leads

8. Setup/install 5-S Visual Control Board for periodic display of progress (can be electronic if necessary)

9. Prepare training materials for different levels, and integrate this training with regular job training as well

10. Provide basic awareness and training on 5-S to employees of selected areas on a pilot basis. This will allow for fine tuning of the training and delivery of the same

Implementing First S - Sort

1. Group decides a day for fortnightly meeting

2. Group prepares an activity chart for the first 15 days (for display on 5-S Board)

3. Take photographs of the 'as is' situation (and display on board)

4. Segregate and remove items that are no longer useful from the work area. Then sort the remaining into needed and un-needed items / documents

5. Put Red Tags on un-needed items and documents, make sure the Red Tags are properly filled out

6. Evaluate Red Tagged items

7. Move Red Tagged items from the work area, start creating an electronic list of such items as well

8. Review progress fortnightly

9. Prepare activity chart for next 15 days (replacing old chart on the 5-S board)

10. Take photographs after first S implementation and display on the board

11. Evaluate and document the benefits from the first S implementation

12. Display on the board for everyone to see, and move to second S

Implementing Second S - Store

1. Take photographs of the work area before start of the second S

2. Classify and codify each item and document left after removal of Red Tag items

3. Decide on the best place for storage for each item and document (you will need to study the usage and replenishment cycles to decide quantity to store)

4. Ensure it is easy to see the available quantity and minimum and maximum levels

5. Provide additional storage if needed

6. Label the storage area (and use visual aids if necessary) for easy identification of each item

7. Use signboards for easy identification of storage location

8. Place the right items in the right locations

9. Maintain electronic record of storage items/ documents for easy traceability

10. Take photographs after items have been stored properly

11. Evaluate and document the benefits from implementation of second S

12. Display benefits on the 5-S Board for everyone to see, and move to third S

Implementing Third S - Shine

1. Photograph the work area before starting the third S

2. Decide on what, when, how, and who should clean every area in the work place

3. Procure necessary materials and supplies for cleaning

4. Identify a place for keeping cleaning materials and supplies

5. Start cleaning and inspect as you go. Check for any anomalous conditions that might exist on equipment, and machinery in the work place

6. Decide on corrective actions for anomalies observed during cleaning inspection (or bring the anomalies to the attention of the right authority)

7. Display anomalies found and corrective actions, on 5-S Board

8. Take photographs after cleaning and display on board

9. Display benefits of cleaning on 5-S Board, and move to fourth S

Implementing the Fourth S - Standardize

1. Prepare the procedure for doing the first three S's with enough detail and graphics, to illustrate how to do each step. Detail should be adequate to ensure different people are able to produce identical results. For example, a procedure on conducting 5-S in ice-cream extrusion should produce same and repeatable results when conducted by different members of a production team

2. Create standard checklists and documents associated with 5-S

3. Train internal auditors and make sure their audits are consistent

4. Set up standard calendars and schedules for periodic 5-S Audit to occur in all work areas

5. Display scores on 5-S Boards in all departments

6. Make sure the corrective action list is created and consistently displayed on each 5-S Board

7. Move on to the fifth S

Implementing the Fifth S - Sustain

1. The Leadership and Management of the organization must review progress on a periodic basis (monthly, then quarterly, moving to bi-annually as the habits take root)

2. Ensure adequate training is in place for all levels to assure a running start

3. Add 5-S as an integral part of the job description across the organization

4. Discuss 5-S successes at staff meetings and department meetings

5. Recognize individual and team efforts, reward appropriately

6. Make sure groups share ideas on how they are faring with 5-S in an open sharing and networking atmosphere

7. Add 5-S implementation road maps, and progress to the company's intranet so all employees can see what is happening

8. Generate reports to show the monetary advantage the organization has gained through 5-S implementation

Chapter 10

Role of 5-S in Lean and Quality

Lean cannot happen without being clean.

This we can say because before going lean (in manufacturing or services), the waste in processes and products needs to be identified. Lean cannot be accomplished if there are layers of stuff that conceal the waste. These layers might be things such as routine daily work that keeps everyone busy, stacks of paper, dust, grime or other time wasting activities such as meetings that are no longer needed. Why does wasteful activity happen despite our knowing that these are bad? Well, the answer is that no one does these things on purpose. These often happen because of past routines / procedures and trapper habits. Believe it or not, we are prisoners of our habits and this causes us to do things without thinking. In the end, waste accumulates and we become blind to the same. 5-S causes one to pause and think differently by asking "Do I really need this?"

Quality improvement requires:

Cleanliness and Orderliness

To improve quality one has to understand what the non-conformances (known or potential) are; then determine the causes for the same. This requires clarity and a good understanding of cause and effect. Here again if layers of stuff conceal the non-conformance and their underlying causes, one cannot even start on the journey of quality improvement.

Sort

To be clean, one has to first sort what is needed and what is not. Human tendency is to postpone decisions and when the time comes to decide whether to discard things or keep them, the tendency with most people is to try and hang on to things. Why? Because, one may need them at sometime.

This can defeat the entire effort. When such thinking sets in, the following questions can help:

- ► When was the last time we used this file/item?
- ► Why does this file/item need to be in this place? Are we concerned that it may get lost if we store it?

- ▸ What will happen if the file / item vanishes?
- ▸ What function will come to a stand still ?
  Try living without it for some time.

Store

The next step in becoming clean is to store things in their right place in the right order. The 80/20 rule can be useful in deciding how to store. According to this rule, only 20% of the things we usually have are needed very often. The rest are not.

A good rule of thumb in designing storage systems is to adopt the rule of 2. This rule is made of 2 parts and these are:

1. **It should take only 2 steps to store the right thing in its right place and it should happen in 2 minutes or less.**
2. **To retrieve what is stored, it should take less than 2 minutes and less than 2 steps.**

This simple rule, when followed, can make storing fast and effective. It also directly enables achievement of better quality results, since delays often cause people to take short cuts which compromises quality.

Shine

The idea behind 'shine' is to increase the signal to noise ratio; this ensures what is important is not lost in the background or in the noise and daily grind of activities. In the manufacturing world, it literally means to shine an object or machine, making it look like new. In the services world, this can take the meaning of visiting the service or operation to see how it is performing. Such an observation can also be of value in spotting waste and prevents taking any unwanted steps that may have become part of routine operations.

Further, a clean operation goes a long way in sending the right messages to employees and customers alike. It tells them that the process owners care and are doing a diligent job. It builds quality at little to no cost. This can help in winning customers and building loyalty. Ask yourself, if two restaurants are equal in all respects and one is cleaner than the other, which one would you rather go to? Junk attracts more junk that is the way trash piles up. This trash has an immediate and direct bearing on quality and in many situations is a safety hazard.

Standardize

To have lean operations, the amount of inventory carried should be minimum. This inventory can comprise of processes, parts, computers, files, people, information, service, manuals, service tools, just about everything.

Moreover, imagine how difficult life can become if there is no standardization, for example, say one brand of car has the clutch on the left pedal and brake in the middle, while another brand has clutch in the middle and brake pedal on the left?

Despite the obvious advantages of standardization, many companies and organizations do not pay attention to this simple concept. For example, one airline company which operates across the country has 9 different types of planes, while another offers an identical service by using only 2 types of planes. The latter, has to carry fewer spares, their crew can easily work with both planes since they do not need multiple certifications, repairs and maintenance are easy to carryout, no wonder it is among the more profitable in the country.

It should be understood that gains from the first 3-Ss

(Sort, Store, Shine) can be completely lost if standardization is not adopted. Lack of standardization leads to variation which is the enemy of quality.

Sustain

It is important to sustain changes until the new habits become natural. Not doing so can result in losing the benefits from the first 4-Ss.

Chapter 11

Major Pitfalls in 5-S Implementation

▶ Start with slogan and end with slogan – many companies are good at kicking off initiatives, amidst a lot of hoopla and slogans, however lack the focus and constancy of purpose to see them through. Why? It is easy to get started on something new because it creates an adrenaline rush. The real champions are ones who keep on going and see things through.

▶ 5-S is considered as once in a year cleaning exercise – this happens when 5-S is thought of as a periodic event rather than adopting it as part of standard work that gets done regularly.

▶ Attitude that cleaning is not my job is a pitfall that occurs particularly in organizations where a hierarchical system is deeply entrenched. Such attitudes make 5-S difficult to sustain, and it will quickly be undone despite getting a good start.

▶ Obsession and attachment with old unwanted items/documents – hesitant to throw them out – this tendency has its roots in the comfort zone we create for ourselves. At a deeper level, it is usually the fear of change that keeps people stay put with such items.

When not addressed properly, this obsession can surface after the launch of 5-S in the company, and defeat any change effort from taking root. It is very costly (more important than the apparent monetary cost from lost time is the loss of credibility that organization's leaders and managers suffer – the cost of which cannot be measured easily) to go through the launch only to find that key stake holders are not going to adopt the new and improved practices.

Assuming that 5-S can be implemented in 5 days unless you are a tiny shop with a handful of people, this is a sign of over-confidence coming from arrogance, and/or a lack of experience. Doing 5-S properly needs some fore thought, and planning. Above all a commitment to adopt it as a way of life in the organization.

► Our office / factory is already clean and there is no need for 5-S implementation – well this might be a good thought, however, in the spirit of continuous improvement, one needs to benchmark your own and other leading organizations looking for opportunities to do better. Stagnation sets in when complacency about continuous improvement takes root. Then it is easy to fall behind as other organizations (or competition) move ahead.

Case Studies

Chapter 12

Case Study
Medicine Cabinet in a Hospital

Background

This case study is from an assisted living facility where patients stay during recovery periods. In most cases, family members can also spend the night with patients, as such this facility serves as a temporary home for patients.

At the facility, it was reported that there were several incidents of missed, incorrect and expired medications being administered to residents. Further, it was suspected that substances that should not be there were also finding their way into the facility. This could be very risky and the facility management was very concerned about accidental usage of such substances. More over, there were complaints that the storage space was too small and more cabinets were needed.

A random audit of the medication cabinet revealed the following :
- Presence of mineral oil

- Expired medications
- Unreadable labels on medications

It was decided to perform 5-S in the facility starting with the medication cabinets for each room. There were a total of 155 rooms in the facility and the staff was trained to do 5-S in a short 3 hour session, followed by a 3 day Kaizen Blitz to clear up all the cabinets. A team of 5 employees was chartered with the task.

Results

As the Kaizen blitz started with 5-S, many staff members would hesitate to decide what to do with the objects / substances found in the cabinets – they wanted to keep them, pending a decision, rather than discard the objects. The Kaizen leader insisted that the decision be made right on the spot, Keep or Discard. As per the existing rules there should be nothing in the medication cabinet other than the patient's medicines. It was okay to have a prescription and over the counter drugs, but nothing else.

The staff was instructed to document the contents and track the time it took to do 5-S. It is of interest to note that 80% of the contents in the cabinet were of low usage. Besides, the money spent on about 70% of the medications was wasted due to excessive dosages being ordered, and the medications sat on the shelf past their expiry dates. In fact some medications were dated as far back as 1998. In addition, the staff also found medication for dogs and birds in the same cabinet. Another notable finding was the presence of mineral oil and solvents, both of which, if swallowed could be dangerous to health.

The summary results are as shown below:

Statistics on medicine cabinet 5-S:

Numbers of unique items	33
Non-medication items	4
Medications for pets	2
No. of expired items	11
No. of prescription medications	7

Cost estimates:

Cost of medications discarded	$ 893.00
Total cost of medications	$ 1277.00

Time duration of 5-S:

Max. time for any patient	44 minutes
Shortest time for any patient	21 minutes

Contents of cabinet by use frequency:

High frequency use items	6
Medium frequency use items	3
Low frequency use items	24

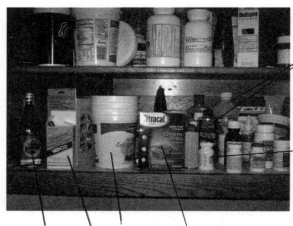

Solvent

Vitamins, pain killers and anti-acid all mixed in the same shelf

Oil Medication for dog Empty food containers Prescribed medication found

NOTE: Pictures of the after condition are not available since patient names were put on the respective cabinets, and privacy guidelines prevent us from sharing such information.

Chapter 13

Case Study
Computer Desktop in Office

Background

When 5-S training was conducted in an organization, the IT professionals also attended the same. Many of them wondered how 5-S would apply to them. We suggested they look at their work areas and determine what had been accumulating.

They returned with the following:
1. Folders and files piling up on the desktop
2. Images that were rarely used had taken up disk space
3. Files were hard to find because often they had to run search routines to find files

Actions after training was completed

After 5-S training, several IT professionals felt that the first thing they would like to clean up was their desktops.

A survey revealed there were an average of 89 files or folder icons on desktops within the department. Considerable time was being lost in just finding the required files. Besides, it was felt that there could also be several files/folders that should have been deleted, but were still there. Everyone agreed that the clean up would help speed the backing up process and also simplify their lives by making files easy to find rather than having to use the 'search' feature in Explorer.

An 80/20 guideline was used which basically meant that 80% of the files they had on the desktops were not required. These could be completely deleted or moved to their respective folders. Then the desktop would be left with about 20% of the files.

The results from an individual's desktop are as follows:

Statistics on files on desktop:

Total files before 5-S	83
After 5-S	17
Files pending decision	3
Files completely deleted	19
Files removed from desktop	39

This individual also reported a 34% (14.6 Gigabytes) reduction in storage space and over 9 minutes of time saving in backing up of the files on a daily basis.

There were 136 professionals who took part in the exercise across the company – you can calculate the projected savings based on this report of a typical IT professional's desktop:

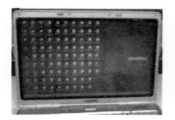 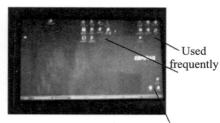

Used frequently

Before: Over 80 icons on desktop not in any logical order

After: 17 most useful icons on desktop

Three are pending decision

Chapter 14

Case Study

Space Management in a Motel Chain

Background

A motel chain was on a rapid growth curve and wanted to increase capacity at each of its motels. Studies on asset utilization showed that the chain lagged behind the best in the industry by about 25% in terms of the number of rental rooms per acre of land. This provided an impetus to make change happen. However, the question was what needed to be changed? One option was to build more rooms where possible.

A random sample of 4 motels showed that up to 17% of the available rooms were being used for storage rather than for generating rental income. A project to make improvements was undertaken with an initial goal of reducing storage space to 12% or less in Phase I; which would be much less expensive than adding more rooms. This 5-S study is a part of the project undertaken to achieve that goal.

Educating Management on Lean

Since the motel chain owners had already experienced the pain of waste and the pressure of competition, they were receptive to any idea that would help improve their operations. A one day executive session on principles of "Lean" was conducted, during which the 7 Wastes of Services and 5-S were discussed. After this session, the senior staff consented to form a small team that would drive 5-S across the organization (226 motels).

Driving 5-S

The 5-S Corporate Team (5-SCT) laid out performance criteria for 5-S compliance within the company. They identified the following dimensions for every location to track and deliver on. Each of the Ss was tracked using a 3 point simple scale as shown below:

Sort

1. Unusable and expired items mixed with items of routine use
2. Excessive quantity of usable items
3. Items in storage are only of the right type and the right quantity

Store

1. Items are hard to find and when found hard to retrieve, and/or wrong items are in storage. No labels indicating what is stored where. It takes more than 3 attempts and over 5 minutes to find things
2. Items are some what hard to find and retrieve. Labels exist for some items
3. Easy to find and retrieve. Labels exist for all items and things are located in 1 minute or even less

Shine

1. Required items are covered with dust or grime to the point that labels are not readable
2. Required items are dirty but labels can be read from a distance of 2 feet
3. Items are clean, there is no dirt or grime and labels can be read from a distance of 4 or more feet

Standardize

1. No schedule and assignments in place for routine 5-S or housekeeping activities
2. One of the two exists; schedule or assignments
3. Responsibilities are assigned and a schedule exists to perform 5-S regularly

Sustain

1. No 5-S metrics exist and it is not on the management's agenda to drive this in their organization

2. 5-S metrics exist, however, management does not discuss this or hold anyone accountable for 5-S in their work area

3. 5-S metrics exist and management routinely monitors performance to these metrics

Since the whole organization was new to Lean and 5-S, the 5-SCT laid out a deployment plan and provided each of the motel managers with the training and tools to deploy 5-S in their locations. The table below shows the road map for the whole organization as it was created at the beginning of the program in July 2005.

Item No.	Activity/ Goal	Metric	Target date	Comments
1	Training on 5-S for managers	% Complete	Mar. 2006	4 Trainers from 5-SCT to cover all motels
2	Training for practitioners	% Complete	Mar. 2006	As above
3	5-S deployment	Composite score by location and company to be at >=2.5	Jul. 2006	Each motel manager to be held accountable

4	Rate of deployment	Change in score per Month:>=0.2 Starting Oct. 2005	Begin measuring from Sept. 2005	5-SCT to audit and report to management at HQ
5	Available rooms per acre of land	% Reduction in storage space from 17% to 15%	Dec. 2005	As above
6	Available rooms per acre of land	% Reduction in storage space from 15% to 12%	Dec. 2006	As above

Sample Project

The 2nd project that was completed as part of this initiative is presented here. The motel had 129 rooms in all, of which 21 rooms were being used for storage. As the team started to list the things in storage, this is what they found (see items in Description):

No.	Description	Purpose/Use	Rate of use used	% of space
1	Old TVs and VCRs	None applicable	Not	20
2	Furniture: tables, chairs, cabinets, lamp stands	Spare/extra	Low	15

3	Cleaning supplies: brooms, pails/ buckets, mops and cleaning solutions	Cleaning or house keeping	High	15
4	Curtains and drapes	Spare/extra	Low	5
5	Empty cardboard boxes	None	Not applicable	5
6	Abandoned items by previous tenants	Return to owner	Not applicable	10
7	Supplies in cabinets	Snacks and condiments for guests	High	30

As the team did the walk-through in different rooms, they documented the space used and the purpose of each item. All the data is shown in the table above. Next came the task of deciding what to do with each item they found. Since the motel staff had saved the items themselves for future use, they had a hard time agreeing to take a decision on some of them. Their main concern was what will they do if they need them tomorrow?

This resistance is natural and was overcome via letting them decide how much of these materials would they actually need given that the space utilization goals were to be accomplished and were non-negotiable. An additional incentive was created that gave them points on the merit review if they donated items to obtain a tax deduction, with the condition that the donated item would not be ordered within 2 years.

This motel's staff underwent the training program during early September 2005 and by November 2005 they made excellent progress. Their scores were:

	Sort	3.0
	Store	3.0
Average:	Shine	2.5
	Standardize	2.0
	Sustain	1.0

No	Description	Comments*	% of space used before 5-S	% of space used after 5-S
1	Old TVs and VCRs	Donate	20	0
2	Furniture: tables, chairs, cabinets, lamp stands	Keep 10% of existing inventory in stock, donate the rest	15	5
3	Cleaning supplies: brooms, pails/ buckets, mops and cleaning solutions	Re-arrange to use vertical space. Eliminate spreading out on floor	15	10

4	Curtains and drapes	Keep 10% of existing inventory In stock, donate the rest	5	2
5	Empty cardboard boxes	Keep as is	5	5
6	Abandoned items by previous tenants	Inform all guests who stayed in the motel in the last three months, give 1 month grace, then discard/ auction/donate as feasible	10	3
7	Supplies in cabinets	Re-arrange to use space more effectively. Discard unused or expired items**	30	20
		Total:	100	45

* All donated items would qualify for a tax write off.

** See images below, showing cabinet use going from 3 shelves to 2.

Supplies in Cabinets

Before : All items stored randomly and same items in multiple places

Note – all shelves occupied with hardly any space left

Items for Storing

Items to be Discarded

Sort and Store

Duplicate or unusable items found as follows:

Cutlery (plastic)	4 places
Sugar/substitute	3 places
Expired drinks/products	3 places
Lamps/bulbs	8 units
Mini-thermos	1

Store and Shine

All items arranged per usage needs, one shelf completely empty.

In this particular case the percentage of space used for storage was reduced by 55%; Overall for the motel, use of 5-S freed up 12 of the 21 rooms that were being used for storage purposes.

The cost savings (and opportunity for additional revenue) are summarized in the table below:

Outcome from 5-S	One time savings, or avoidance	Additional revenue opportunity	Comments
Donation of surplus items	$2386	Not applicable	None
Freed up 12 rooms for rent	$66,000 (@$5500/room)	$144,000 ($12000/year/room)	$6000 spent on repainting the rooms

Chapter 15

Case Study
5-S for Families
by Mrs. Davorka Filipusic (USA)

Many articles have been written about 5-S programs
and their applications in the business environment. As a
quality professional, I have been involved with
teaching, implementing, supporting, improving or
revitalizing such programs in several manufacturing and
service organizations.

When I started, it didn't occur to me that these
principles would one day have such a significant impact
on my personal life.

My son was born four years ago and because he didn't
come with an instruction manual, the last four years
have been challenging for my husband and me. We had
to get used to our new roles as parents while remaining
full-time working professionals.

As our son grew, so did his needs and space
requirements. One of the biggest challenges we faced
was the increasing clutter in our house that came with
our son's growing assortment of toys, books, games and
whatever else he decided to collect. As the toys became

bigger and bulkier every year and because some of them were dangerous to step on, they started to present a home safety hazard in addition to an aesthetic problem.

Explaining the importance of good housekeeping, organization, safety and recycling to a 4 year old child isn't easy.

However, I realized it was something that should be taught to children at just that age.

A solution was desperately needed, so some decisions had to be made quickly. At the time, I was successfully teaching and implementing a 5-S program in a business environment. This gave me an idea: Why not apply the same principles at home and take back control of my house, while ingraining these fundamentals into my son's daily routine?

Define and Develop

The first thing I had to do was to define and develop a 5-S program for our family in a manner that my four year old son could easily understand and respond to.

The next step was to provide designated areas in the house, as well as tools for organizing and storing items.

This was probably the most challenging part. While thousands of storage solutions are in the market today, our challenge was to find storage elements that would fit well in our home, have an acceptable appearance and be functional and child friendly.

After we settled on the first three S's – sort, set in order and shine – it was time to decide as a family how we were going to standardize (Fourth S) and sustain (Fifth S) activities on a daily basis. To standardize, we cooperated to develop our family's 5-S policy. We also decided that it would apply to each family member.

5-S in your corner:

A corner of the author's house reorganized by 5-S. Note the process maps on the door and the status board on the wall.

The focus of our 5-S program was to quickly identify needless items (clothes, toys, books, CDs, DVDs , mails, magazines) and put them in their designated places while considering recycling or reusing options. All 5-S activities were to be implemented continuously in all areas of the house.

Our objectives were to improve the appearance of our home, contribute to the personal safety of all family members and improve our mental and physical well-being while teaching our child valuable life lessons. To measure and sustain our 5-S activities, we decided that at the end of each day, we would rate our individual 5-S efforts with smiling or frowning face magnets on a special magnetic board.

For children our son's age, using face symbols for feedback was very effective. Our son was very competitive, so he was willing to do anything to avoid being rated with the dreaded frowning face!

Back to Control

Shortly after implementing 5-S, I regained control of the house and everybody in the family, including me, was doing his or her share of daily 5-S activities. My son now applies 5-S steps in whatever he does without any extra effort. It has become part of his daily routine. When someone in the house says "5-S", everybody understands what it means and knows what needs to be done.

Implementing 5-S in your family is an amazing learning experience for kids and parents.

To succeed, all family members must be involved, but parent participation and guidance are especially important. Parents must lead by example. In my case, this was easy because my husband also is a quality professional and he supported the idea from the beginning.

5-S is a lot more than a cleanup project. It is important that both children and adults have fun while doing it and at the same time learn important habits and behaviors, at home. The orderly appearance of your home will improve the quality of your life and lessons learned will remain with your children for years to come.

Reference

1.For a definition of 5-S, see ASQ's glossary at www.asq.org/glossary/f.html.

5-S for Kids and Parents

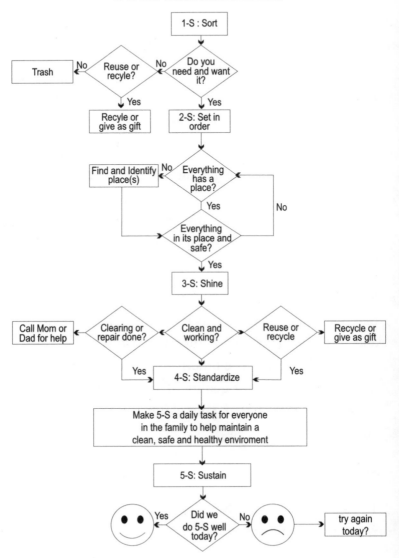

5-S Implementation – Audit Sheet Example

-you may need to change / adapt it to fit your situation

FIRST S- SEIRI or SORT

Serial No	Check Point	Check off		Comments
		Yes	No	
Visual Control				
1	Photographs with dates posted on 5S board			
2	Latest activity chart displayed on 5S board			
3	Team Member/Team Leader/ Convener name posted			
4	Old activity charts and old photographs removed from 5S board			
5	Houses, electrical cables are properly covered & free from safety hazards			
6	Electrical connections and boards are free from safety hazards			
7	Is the floor free from pot holes & uneven surfaces			
8	Is the area conducive for safe movements of people and material and pathways are clearly visible			

9	Are the needed and unneeded items sorted and kept separated			
10	**Fire extinguishers checked for**			
	1 Expiry Date 2 Refilling volume 3 Easy access			
11	**Disposal**			
	1 Is procedure available 2 Frequency for disposal time defined 3 Legal requirements checked			
12	**Responsibilities are assigned for**			
	1 Maintenance of the 5S Board 2 Red Tagging, Shifting of needed items to be used in future, Disposal of items/ Documents 3 Maintenance of safe working environment 4 Maintenance of Records			
13	**Records of benefits available in terms of**			
	1 Extra Space 2 Money Saved 3 Man Power Saved 4 Facilities become Surplus			

SECOND S- SEITON or SET IN ORDER

Serial No	Check Point	Check off		Comments
		Yes	No	
Visual Control				
1	Is the list of needed items to be stored near the place of work (with maximum quantity) is prepared			
2	Are all the items classified & codified			
3	Are specific locations decided for each item/document			
4	Are the decided locations best (minimum movement and safe)			
5	Are responsibilities for various activities defined			
6	Shelf stratification for items/ documents kept in shelf/almirah is done			
7	Whether items have location description			
8	Visual Management Practiced			
	1 Colour Coding 2 Arrow Marks 3 Visual Displays-Signboard 4 Earmarked Danger Zone			

9	**Satisfactory placement of**			
	I Posters 2 Notices 3 Calendars 4 Displays			
10	Are spaces saved because of better storage method			
11	**Are following things orderly**			
	1 Shelves 2 Tables, Chairs, Furniture, and other storage items 3 Cleaning Implements			
12	Are items easily accessible			
Stacking system (illustration - breakable items, Small Vs Large items, Light Vs Heavy items, Combustible Vs Non Combustible)				
13	Are storage of sensitive items done properly (Flammable items, Poisonous items, Acids etc.)			
14	Are storage of Delicate items done properly (Breakable, Fragile, Glass items)			
15	Is time saved because of better storage methods			
16	Are records of benefits available			

THIRD S- SEISO or SHINE

Serial No	Check Point	Check off		Comments
		Yes	No	
General				
1	Are all items/documents covered under cleaning schedule			
2	Is proper drainage system identified and maintained			
3	Have you removed dirt and dust from nooks & corners			
4	Have you removed dirt, dust from (including the side and below portion) 1 Trolley/Stands/Racks 2 Table 3 Chair			
5	Have you removed dirt, dust from doors and windows			
6	Have you removed dust from 1 Fans 2 A/C, water coolers 3 Notice Board			
7	Are cleaning responsibilities defined			

8	Is exhaust and ventilation and light adequate and working			
9	Are trash cans empty regularly			

I - Inventory Items

1	Have you removed all dirt and dust from products, parts, documents and materials			
2	Are machine and machine accessories rust free			
3	Have you removed dirt from inventory shelf/almirah			
4	Have you removed dirt from work in-process inventory			
5	Have you removed dirt from container/pallets used to move items			

II - SPACES

1	Have you removed trash and empty containers from the surrounding of the building			
2	Are all drainage clean			
3	Have you removed dust and dirt and trash, water and oil puddles from floor spaces and walkways			
4	Have you removed dust and dirt from walls, windows, and doors			

5	Have you removed smudges and dust from window glasses			
6	Have you removed dust and dirt from			
	ceilings and beams light tubes and bulbs light fixtures (stands, shades, etc) shelves and worktables			
7	Have you removed oil and trash from walkways and stairwells			
8	Have you removed dirt and grime (handmarks) from the bottoms and corners of pillars and walls			
III Equipments				
	Have you removed dust, dirt, oil and water, oil stems, finger smudges from the			
1	Surrounding of the equipment			
2	Underneath the equipment			
3	Top of the equipment			
4	Equipment sides and covers			
5	Glass displays, such as in oil level gauges or pneumatic pressure Gauges			
6	Inside of the equipment covers and lids			

7	Pneumatic pipes and electrical cables			
8	All switches			
9	Bulbs and tubes			
10	Steps and other surfaces			
11	Jigs fixture and cutting tools			
12	Dies			
13	Measuring and testing instruments			

IV - Office

Have you removed dust from

1	Chair legs			
2	Table bottom			
3	Table and chair bottom structure			
4	Files kept inside and outside the shelves			
5	Top of the shelves/almirah/racks			
6	Inside shelves of the almirah/racks			
7	Computer			
8	Printer			

9	Keyboard			
10	Hard disk and other accessories associated with computer			
11	Side rack			
12	In and out tray, inside of the table drawer			
13	Chairs, sofa pieces, side tables, center table, lamp and lamp shades			
14	Curtains & carpets			

FOURTH S- SEIKETSU or STANDARDIZE

Serial No	Check Point	Check off		Comments
		Yes	No	
Office				
1	Are indent sent for replaceable furniture, files and storage bin			
2	Are repairable furniture sent for repair			
3	Are there any electrical switches/ connections 1- Repairable 2- Replaceable			
4	Are there any abnormalities			

	GENERAL			

1	Have you decided procedure for cleaning (what, how, when) for the following-
	  1 Floors, walls, roofs, window, doors, stairways
	  2 Chairs/sit outs, tables, racks, shelves, almirah
	  3 Computers & accessories
	  4 Fans, lights, AC/Coolers
	  5 Curtains
	  6 Carpet			

2	Is there any defined procedure for the use of fire fighting equipment			
3	Are the people trained for use of fire fighting equipment			
4	Are cables/wires covered and free from safety hazards			
5	Entrance to departments are identified and visible			
6	Is existence of Standard Procedure for each "S" available			

FIFTH S- SHITSUKE or SUSTAIN

Serial No	Check Point	Check off		Comments
		Yes	No	
Promotional Activity				
1	Is there an organization to drive the movement			
2	Are promotional meetings taking place			
3	Records of such meetings available			
4	Whether 5-S Posters, competitors arranged for wider participation and creating awareness on 5-S among people			
5	Are there awards for best department			
6	Are funds available when required for 5-S implementation			
7	Is employees training program schedule drawn			
8	Are employees trained on 5-S as per schedule			
9	Are success stories published			

10	Are benefits communicated to the people			
11	Do business leaders and managers walk the talk			
12	Do business leaders and managers empower, encourage and enable their employees to take ownership and drive 5-S on their own			

Wisdom Village Publications Pvt Ltd
Knowledge is information. Wisdom is transformation.

| Broom & Groom MRP Rs 195/-(HB) Kiran Bedi, Pavan Choudary | Art of Getting People To say Yes MRP Rs 200/- Arvinder Brara | When you are Sinking become a Submarine MRP Rs 195/- Pavan Choudary | TV News Writing Made Easy for Newcomers MRP Rs 150/- Ravi M. Khanna | Let go MOM MRP Rs 150/- Shivi Dua |

— Pavan Choudary —

| Chanakya's Political Wisdom MRP Rs 100/-(HB) | Confucius' Social Wisdom MRP Rs 100/-(HB) | Kabir's Spiritual Wisdom MRP Rs 100/-(HB) | Success Sutras for the 21st Century Set of 3 Books(HB) in a Box MRP Rs 290/- |

| Healing in your Hands (Acupressure) MRP Rs 250/- Dr. Anand Verma | The Rx Factor (Pharmaceutical Marketing-Reprint) MRP Rs 125/- Pavan Choudary | Rendezvous with God: Modern Day Miracles MRP: Rs150.00 Compiled by Abhilasha Agarwal and Shreeja Mohatta Jhawar | Arise Awake MRP Rs 225/- Dr. P.V. Vaidyanathan | Setbacks to Comebacks MRP Rs 150/- Nishit Lal |

ORDER YOUR COPY. ON BULK ORDER AVAIL SPECIAL DISCOUNT
CONTACT -+91 98108 00469, wvpdindia@gmail.com